anythink

D0699319

our world of faith
Islam

by Holly Wallace

NEW
FOREST
PRESS

An Hachette Company

First published in the United States by
New Forest Press, an imprint of Octopus Publishing Group Ltd

www.octopusbookusa.com

Copyright © Octopus Publishing Group Ltd 2012

Published by arrangement with Black Rabbit Books
PO Box 784, Mankato, MN 56002

Printed and bound in the USA

16 15 14 13 12 1 2 3 4 5

Publisher: Tim Cook   Editor: Margaret Parrish   Designer: Steve West

We would like to thank: Jean Coppendale, Honor Head, Plan UK and Plan International, and Dr. Hasan, Assistant Director, The Muslim Education Trust, London, England.

With special thanks to Hambali and his family

Library of Congress Cataloging-in-Publication Data

Wallace, Holly, 1961-
Islam: Hambali's Story / by Holly Wallace.
p. cm. – (Our world of faith)
Includes index.
Summary: "Using a first-person narrative, explains the beliefs, customs, and festivals of Islam. Explains the clothing, traditions, food, historical writings, holy days, and holy places that define Muslims. Includes a map to show where Islam originated"–Provided by publisher.
ISBN 978-1-84898-612-1 (hardcover, library bound)
1. Islam–Juvenile literature. I. Title.
BP161.3.W355 2013
297–dc23
2012003254

Picture credits
t = top, b = bottom, c = center, l = left, r = right,
OFC = outside front cover, OBC = outside back cover

Alamy: 12main, 13t, 14, 15t. Art Directors & Trip Photo Library: 11c, 13b, 15c, 23t, 29t. Corbis: 9t, 9b, 31b, 11t, 17b, 19t, 21t, 25c, 28b, 31br. Getty Images: 26. Plan UK and Plan International: 1, 2, 4b, 5all, 6 all, 7t, 7c, 10all, 11b, 14all, 16t, 17t & c, 18t, 19c, 20all, 22t, 24all, 26t, 31tl. Shutterstock: 7b, 21c, 23b, 28, 30t. Superstock: 19b, 27b. World Religions PL/Christine Osborne: 16b, 21b, 22b, 25t, 25b, 27t.

Contents

I am a Muslim 4-5

My family........................... 6-7

LEARN MORE: What is Islam? 8-9

What I believe 10-11

LEARN MORE: A special book 12-13

The Five Pillars of Islam........................... 14-15

Saying prayers 16-17

Where I worship........................... 18-19

The month of fasting........................... 20-21

Eid ul-Fitr—the end of the fast................. 22-23

Other festivals 24-25

Special occasions 26-27

LEARN MORE: Holy places 28-29

Glossary........................... 30-31

Index........................... 32

Words that appear in **bold** are explained in the glossary.

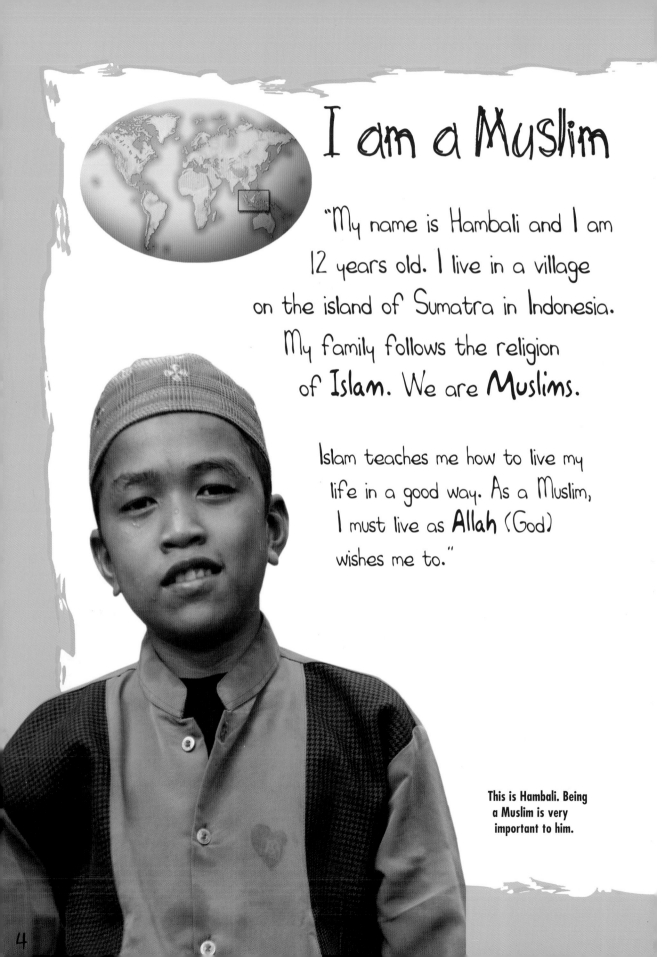

I am a Muslim

"My name is Hambali and I am 12 years old. I live in a village on the island of Sumatra in Indonesia. My family follows the religion of Islam. We are **Muslims**.

Islam teaches me how to live my life in a good way. As a Muslim, I must live as **Allah** (God) wishes me to."

This is Hambali. Being a Muslim is very important to him.

Hambali's house has a low, sloping roof, which helps to keep the rooms cool in the very hot weather.

"The name of my village is Ladong. I live here with my family. We live in a small house."

"Everyone in my village is a Muslim. All the girls wear scarves to cover their hair. I wear a small cap most of the time."

Many Muslim girls wear headscarves called hijabs. They also wear long skirts or pants.

This is a large mosque in Indonesia. Most mosques are decorated with patterns.

"I worship in a building called a mosque. There is a small mosque in the village where I pray every day and a much bigger one just outside the village."

My family

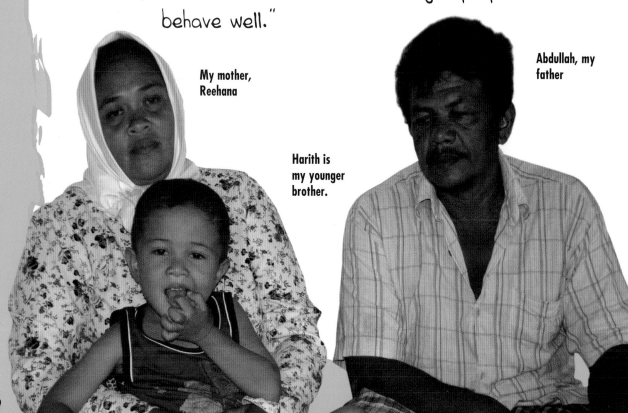

"I live with my mother and father, my sister, who is sixteen, and my little brother, who is three years old. Muslims believe that looking after our families and other Muslims is very important.

Being a good Muslim means respecting everyone and living honestly. I follow the **Qur'an** and try to follow the way the **Prophet Muhammad** lived. He taught people how to behave well."

My mother, Reehana

Harith is my younger brother.

Abdullah, my father

Hambali's family lives in the countryside. They keep chickens and ducks on their land.

"I go to school in the village and enjoy reading. At home I take care of the chickens and ducks."

"My parents have taught me to be kind, to have good manners, and not to steal or lie. They are teaching my little brother the same things."

Muslims believe it is important to love and respect your family because they care for you.

This tasty dish made of eggs, potatoes, and vegetables is halal. Muslims are not allowed to eat pork.

"At mealtimes we eat together. The food we eat must be **halal**. We can eat all fruit and vegetables and some meat and fish."

LEARN MORE: What is Islam?

- Islam is a religion that began in Arabia, now called Saudi Arabia.

- Islam was brought to the world by the Prophet Muhammad about 1,400 years ago.

Saudi Arabia

- Muslims live all over the world.

WORLD MAP

UK

US

Pakistan

Bangladesh

India

Nigeria

AFRICA

Indonesia

Australia

- In the **Arabic** language the word for God is "Allah."

- Indonesia, where Hambali lives, has the largest number of Muslims, followed by India and Bangladesh.

- Some countries, such as Saudi Arabia and Pakistan, are mainly Muslim. But many Muslims also live in the US, Europe, and Australia.

These young Muslim girls are reading passages from the Qur'an in Nigeria, a country in Africa.

- Islam is the fastest growing religion in the world.

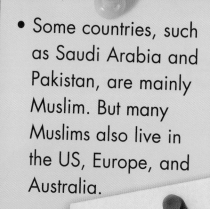

A mosque usually has a dome and tall towers called minarets.

- Muslims make up nearly 20 percent of the world's population.

- Muslims may pray anywhere, but many go to a special place of worship called a mosque, or masjid.

What I believe

"Muslims believe in one God. We call God Allah and worship Him. We believe that Allah created the world and everything in it.

Muslims obey Allah's wishes as they are explained in the Qur'an and follow His guidance in all parts of their lives."

Hambali enjoys reading the Qur'an and learning all the stories in it.

The story of how Islam began

"Muhammad was born in **Makkah**. His parents died when he was young. Later, he became a rich **merchant**, but spent a lot of time praying and thinking about life.

Today, Makkah is a modern city in Saudi Arabia. In Muhammad's time, it was an important center for merchants and traders.

This is the holy cave of Hira, near Makkah. It is visited by pilgrims from around the world.

One day, Muhammad was in a cave when a messenger from Allah came to him. This was the **Angel Jibril**, who began to give him messages from Allah.

Over many years, Muhammad was given lots of different messages from Allah. These messages were later put together in the Qur'an."

The Qur'an is the holy book of Islam. To Muslims it is the most important book in the world.

LEARN MORE: A special book

- The Qur'an is the holy book of Islam. It very important because Muslims believe that it is the word of Allah.

- The Qur'an is a guide to help all Muslims live according to Allah's wishes.

The Qur'an is written in Arabic. Many Muslims have to learn Arabic so that they can read it.

- The Qur'an is divided into 114 chapters, called surahs, and is made up of thousands of verses.

- Understanding the Qur'an and its teachings can take a lifetime.

- Words from the Qur'an are often written above the doorway of a mosque.

- Many Muslims read the Qur'an every day after morning prayers.

Mosques are usually decorated with patterns and words in Arabic because pictures or statues of Allah are not allowed. These words say "Qur'an" in Arabic.

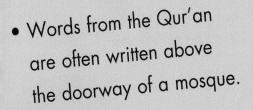

- Many Muslims cover their copy of the Qur'an with a cloth to keep it clean and protect it from damage.

Some Muslims keep the Qur'an on a high shelf and will not put another book above it.

The Qur'an is treated with great respect by all Muslims. It is often placed on a wooden stand to be read.

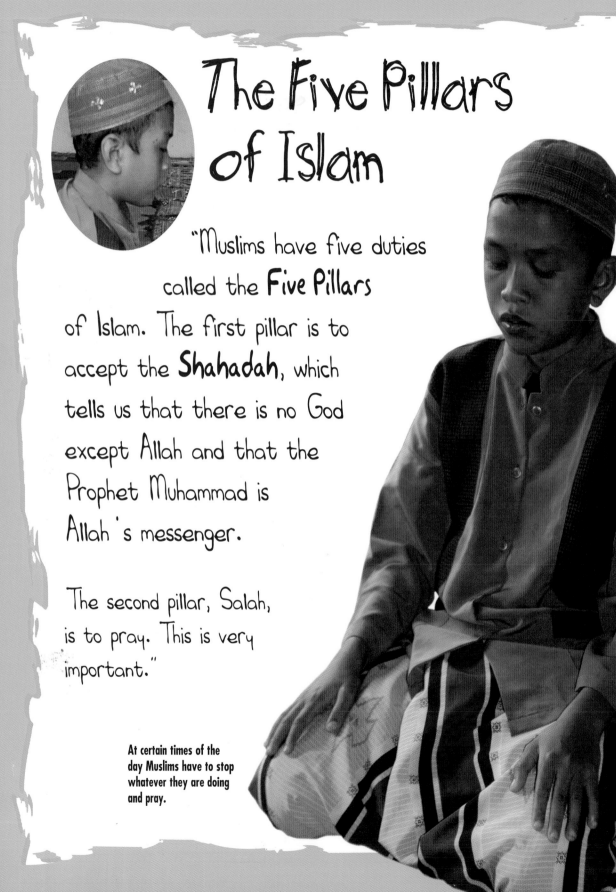

The Five Pillars of Islam

"Muslims have five duties called the **Five Pillars** of Islam. The first pillar is to accept the **Shahadah**, which tells us that there is no God except Allah and that the Prophet Muhammad is Allah's messenger.

The second pillar, Salah, is to pray. This is very important."

At certain times of the day Muslims have to stop whatever they are doing and pray.

All Muslims are expected to give some of their money to the poor every year.

"The third pillar, Zakah, is to give money to the poor. There is a collection box outside my mosque where we put money for the needy."

"The fourth pillar, Sawm, is to **fast** for the month of **Ramadan**. Fasting teaches us to be grateful for what we have."

Children fast for the first time when they are eight years old, but only for a few days. The full fast starts at 12 to 14 years old.

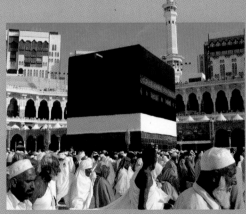

Millions of Muslims make a pilgrimage to the Ka'bah in the city of Makkah. Every Muslim who is able goes there at least once.

"The fifth pillar is to make the **pilgrimage** to Makkah. This is called the **Hajj**. I will do this when I am old enough."

15

Saying prayers

"I say my prayers five times a day. I say them early in the morning, at noon, in the middle of the afternoon, at dusk, and later at night. A man called a **mu'adhin** calls us to prayer.

Prayer is very important in Islam. When I pray, I believe I am talking to Allah."

The mu'adhin usually calls from the top of a tall tower, called a minaret, at the mosque.

Most mosques have a place where Muslims can wash before they pray.

"Before I pray I wash in a special way called **wudu**. First, I wash my face, then my hands and arms up to my elbows. Finally, I wipe my head and wash my feet up to my ankles."

"As I say my prayers, I have to stand, bow, kneel, and then bend forward and touch the ground with my forehead."

All Muslims must perform the same series of actions when they pray to Allah.

Muslims often put a mat on the ground, so the place where they say their prayers is as clean as possible.

"There are no chairs or stools in a mosque. Instead, the floor is covered with mats, where Muslims kneel to pray."

Where I worship

"Every day, I go to the small wooden mosque near my home to say my prayers. On Fridays, I go to the bigger mosque outside my village for special prayers.

After prayers, the **Imam** sometimes gives a talk. He may tell a story from the Qur'an or he may speak about something that has happened in my village."

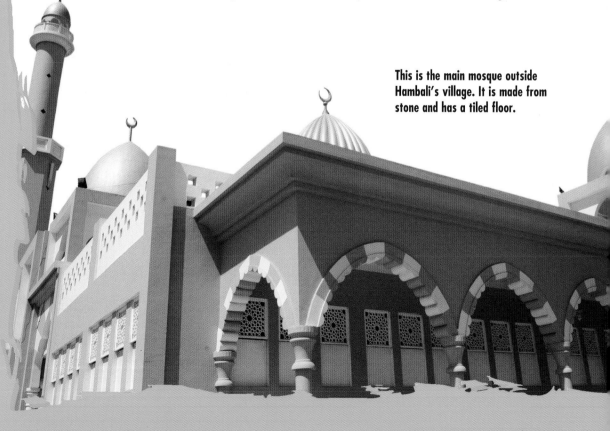

This is the main mosque outside Hambali's village. It is made from stone and has a tiled floor.

Muslims remove their shoes before prayer wherever they are to keep the place of worship clean.

"Everyone takes his or her shoes off before entering the mosque. If many people are there, it can take a long time to find my shoes again."

"I go to a special school at the mosque. Here, I learn the Qur'an and how to say my prayers in Arabic."

Hambali and other boys and girls are taught to read and understand the Qur'an at the mosque school.

An arch in one of the walls of the mosque is called a mihrab. This shows the direction of Makkah.

"Muslims pray facing the direction of the Ka'bah in Makkah. Prayers are usually led by the Imam, a man who has studied Islam for many years."

The month of fasting

"Every year, Muslims have to fast for a month. This month is called Ramadan.

This is a special time for Muslims because it was when Allah sent down the first words of the Qur'an to the Prophet Muhammad. Fasting teaches us to be grateful for what we have."

Children do not have to fast as strictly as adults. When Hambali is a teenager he will have to fast during the day for a whole month.

The mosque has charts that give the times of sunset and sunrise each day.

"During Ramadan, we go without food or drink from sunrise to sunset. I fast for some of the time."

"At sunset, we have a sip of water and eat some dates to end the fast for that day. Then we go to the mosque to pray."

Muslims eat dates during Ramadan because this is what the Prophet Muhammad did when he fasted.

This Muslim family is eating for the first time after the day's fast. Muslims are allowed to eat any halal food they like after sunset.

"After prayers, we have our only real meal of the day. Because he is so young, my brother can eat and drink a little during the day."

21

Eid ul-Fitr—the end of the fast

"When Ramadan is over we celebrate with a festival called **Eid ul-Fitr.** This is a very happy time, especially since I get a vacation from school! The festival is to thank Allah for giving us the strength to fast for a month."

These children are holding ketupat. This is a special rice dish eaten during the festival of Eid ul-Fitr.

Adults and children often wear new clothes to the mosque on the first day of Eid ul-Fitr.

"In the morning I go to the mosque to pray. People who live in the city come home to be with their families, so it can get very crowded."

"After prayers, I ask Allah and my parents to forgive me for all I have done wrong. I swap cards and candies with my friends."

Many children make cards to celebrate Eid ul-Fitr. They give the cards to their family and friends.

Many Muslims prepare the food the day before the festival starts. Dishes such as this halal meat curry with rice and vegetables are popular.

"Then we have our big family meal of rice dumplings served with vegetables, curry, and meat, followed by a sweet cake, which is my favorite."

Other festivals

"Another special festival is **Eid ul-Adha**. This is when we remember the story of the Prophet **Ibrahim** and his son **Ismail**.

Allah asked Ibrahim to **sacrifice** his beloved son Ismail to prove his obedience. Just as Ibrahim was about to do this, Allah stopped him. Allah was pleased that Ibrahim was willing to obey him, so he let Ismail live."

Eid ul-Adha is a time to share and give money and gifts to the poor.

Men from Hambali's village bless goats ready to be given to the poor during Eid ul-Adha.

"Eid ul-Adha takes place on the last day of the Hajj. After prayers, we visit the poor and give them gifts."

"Islam does not have a holiday for the New Year, but we celebrate it in my village. We dress up and some of our relatives come to visit."

This Indonesian girl is holding a lighted candle as part of the celebration for the New Year.

Muhammad's birthday is not an official holiday, but in some countries Muslims hold street parades and special celebrations.

"The birthday of Muhammad is called **Mawlid al-Nabi.** On this day, the Imam tells stories about how brave and wise Muhammad was."

Special occasions

"There are lots of special occasions in a Muslim's life. They begin as soon as we are born. The parents put a little honey on the baby's tongue so that the first thing the baby tastes is sweet."

In some parts of the world Muslims organize group weddings. This helps to keep the cost down for poorer families who cannot afford a very expensive wedding.

The first words a baby hears are the most important Muslim beliefs.

"When a baby is born the father whispers a prayer in its ear. When the baby is a week old, it is named."

"A wedding takes place at the bride's home or in the mosque. The couple signs a paper that sets out the rules of their marriage."

A couple getting married reads from the Qur'an as part of the ceremony.

Muslims are always buried and never cremated. All graves must face the Ka'bah, in the holy city of Makkah.

"When someone dies their body is buried in a grave. This usually takes place the day after the person has died."

27

LEARN MORE: *Holy places*

- The holiest places in the world for Muslims are Makkah and **Madinah**. Both cities are in Saudi Arabia.

SAUDI ARABIA
- Madinah
- Makkah

- Makkah is the site of the Ka'bah. This is the holiest building for Muslims.

- The Ka'bah is a stone platform built by the Prophet Ibrahim and his son Ismail for Allah.

- The Ka'bah is covered by a black cloth to protect it.

- Male pilgrims making the Hajj have to wear white cotton clothes. This is so that they all look the same before Allah.

Pilgrims from all over the world visit the Ka'bah. Many walk a long way to reach the holy site. They are offered food on the way.

- Because many people did not like what the Prophet Muhammad was teaching, Allah told him to leave Makkah and go to Madinah. This is where the first Muslim community started.

The Mosque of the Prophet Muhammad in Madinah is where the tomb of Muhammad lies.

Glossary

A Halal meal

Allah The word for God in the Arabic language.

Angel Jibril An Angel of Allah, known as Gabriel to Christians. Jibril brought the message from Allah to the Prophet Muhammad and to all the other prophets.

Arabic The religious language of Islam. Muslims pray in Arabic and the Qur'an is written in Arabic.

Cremated When a dead person's body is burned.

Eid ul-Adha A festival at which Muslims remember the story of Ibrahim and Ismail. It is celebrated on the last day of the Hajj.

Eid ul-Fitr A festival that celebrates the end of Ramadan, the month of fasting.

Fast To go without food or drink. Muslims fast during the month of Ramadan.

Five Pillars Five duties that Muslims follow in their daily lives.

Hajj The yearly pilgrimage (journey) to Makkah that all Muslims try to make at least once in their lives.

Halal Food that Muslims are allowed to eat. Halal means "allowed."

Hijabs The headscarves Muslim girls wear to cover their hair.

Ibrahim A prophet of Islam. Ibrahim is also known as Abraham and is important to Jews and Christians.

Imam The person who leads the prayers in a mosque.

Islam The name for the religion followed by Muslims.

Ismail A prophet of Islam and the son of Ibrahim. Muslims remember the story of Ibrahim and Ismail at the festival Eid ul-Adha.

Ka'bah The cube-shaped building in Makkah that is the holiest building in Islam.

The Qur'an

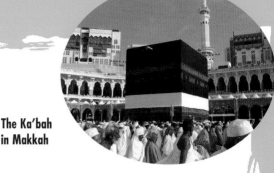

The Ka'bah in Makkah

Madinah The second holiest city of Islam. This is where the Prophet Muhammad died.

Makkah The holiest city of Islam. This is where the Prophet Muhammad was born.

Merchant A person who makes a living by buying and selling goods.

Mawlid al-Nabi The festival that celebrates the Prophet Muhammad's birthday. In Arabic, "mawlid" means "birthday" and "al-Nabi" means "the prophet."

Minarets The towers of a mosque from which the call to prayer is made.

Mu'adhin The person who makes the call to prayer from the mosque.

Muslims People who follow the religion of Islam.

Pilgrimage A journey made to a special religious place.

Prophet Muhammad The last and greatest prophet, or messenger, of Islam.

Qur'an The holy book of Islam containing the teachings that Allah gave to the Prophet Muhammad.

Ramadan The Muslim month during which Muslims fast between sunrise and sunset.

Sacrifice When something is killed as a gift to Allah.

Shahadah The First Pillar of Islam. This is the main belief of Islam.

Wudu A special way of washing that Muslims do before they pray or enter the mosque.

Minarets

Index

A
Allah 4, 10, 24, 30
Angel Jibril 11, 30
Arabia 8
Arabic language 8, 13, 30

B
beliefs 10–11
birth 26, 27
black cloth 28

C
call to prayer 16
celebrations 22–23
chapters of Qur'an 12
clothes 5, 19, 29
collection box 15
community 29
cremated bodies 27, 30

D
dates 21

E
Eid ul-Adha 24–25, 30
Eid ul-Fitr 22–23, 30
end of the fast 22–23

F
families 6–7
fasting 15, 20–21, 22–23, 30
festivals 24–25
five pillars 14–15, 30
food 7, 23, 26
Friday 18

G
God 10
guidance 10, 12

H
Hajj 15, 25, 30
halal 7, 23, 30
headscarves 5
hijabs 5, 30
holy places 28–29

I
Ibrahim 24, 28, 30
Imam 18, 19, 30
Indonesia 4, 8
Islam 4, 8–9, 30
Ismail 24, 28, 30

J
Jibril 11, 30

K
Ka'bah 15, 19, 27, 29, 30
ketupat 22

M
Madinah 28–29, 31
Makkah 11, 15, 19, 27, 28–29, 31
marriage 27
masjid 9
Mawlid al-Nabi 25, 31
merchants 11, 31
mihrab 19
minarets 9, 31
month of fasting 20–21
mosques 5, 9, 13, 18–19
mu'adhin 16, 31
Muhammad 6, 11, 25, 29, 31
Muslim community 29
Muslims 4, 31

N
New Year 25

P
patterns on mosques 5, 13
pilgrimage 11, 15, 29, 31
pork 7
prayer mats 17
prayers 16–17
Prophet Muhammad 6, 11, 25, 29, 31

Q
Qur'an 6, 10–13, 18, 20, 31

R
Ramadan 15, 20–21, 31
respect 7, 13

S
sacrifice 24, 31
Salah 14
Saudi Arabia 8, 28
Sawm 15
Shahadah 14, 31
special occasions 26–27
surahs 12

T
tomb of Muhammad 29

W
washing 17
weddings 26–27
white cotton clothes 29
worship 18–19
wudu 17, 31

Z
Zakah 15